CARL MARIA VON WEBER

DER FREISCHÜTZ

Overture to the Opera
WeV C.7

Edited by/Herausgegeben von
Tim Hüttemeister
Joachim Veit

Ernst Eulenburg Ltd

London · Mainz · Madrid · New York · Paris · Prague · Tokyo · Toronto · Zürich

CONTENTS

Critical edition based on
Carl Maria von Weber. Complete Works
Volume III/5a
© 2017 Schott Music GmbH & Co. KG, Mainz
WGA 1034-10, ISMN 979-0-001-19338-2
Reprinted by permission

© 2019 Ernst Eulenburg & Co GmbH, Mainz
for Europe excluding the British Isles
Ernst Eulenburg Ltd, London
for all other countries

Ernst Eulenburg Ltd
48 Great Marlborough Street
London W1F 7BB

PREFACE

As was his custom, Carl Maria von Weber composed the overture to his three-act opera *Der Freischütz* in May 1820 as the final section of compositional work (except for the Romance later inserted for Ännchen), thus more than a year before the première of the work in Berlin on 18 June 1821. Weber's patience was put to a hard test by the long wait up to the Berlin première, so that in the meantime he already performed individual numbers of the work within private circles. The overture was even, conversely, performed in public: He took copies of the parts along on his trip to northern Germany and Copenhagen during the summer and fall of 1820. Already before the opera's première it was verifiably heard in Halle, Copenhagen, Hamburg, Braunschweig and Dresden.

Apart from the piano reduction (published in October 1821 and offered for sale as a whole, along with single numbers), the overture is the only portion of the work already available in printed parts during Weber's lifetime. After unsuccessful negotiations with Nikolaus Simrock, Weber concluded in October 1822 a publishing contract with the Berlin publisher Adolph Martin Schlesinger and delivered the engraver's model to him the same month. The parts appeared at the end of 1822.

These parts, in addition to the extant autograph score and eight manuscript copies of the work authorised by Weber, are the relevant sources for the overture. Since from the print of the parts it cannot be clearly determined which changes (primarily articulation and slur placement) go back to the composer, the present edition follows as faithfully as possible the edition's main source, the extant autograph preserved in the Staatsbibliothek zu Berlin (siglum: Mus. ms. autogr. C. M. v. Weber 7).

The present score is not intended to be a practical edition, but documents, in accordance with the guidelines of the Weber Complete Edition, not only the composer's notational habits, but in many cases the specific details of the incomplete secondary layer (for instance, bb. 61ff., 171ff. 202ff. or 279ff.), representatively notated only in the upper part (e.g., bb. 59ff., 209ff.), not unequivocally (bb. 243ff.) and occasionally also contradictorily (bb.181ff., 209ff., Fl. and Vl., bb. 243ff., horns). Here, the editors have intervened only very conservatively, opting largely to preserve the original notation showing Weber as calculatedly composing with very subtle tonal nuances.

Editorial interventions made from the sources are shown in ( ), independent editorial recommendations in [ ]. Parts only indicated by *colla parte* markings are included in the signs ⌈ and ⌉. The markings placed above the music text indicate a change of page from left to right ⊤ or a page break in the autograph ⊤⌈ – in many cases it becomes clear why such entries as dynamics or articulation unexpectedly break off at such places. In the case of solo indications, Weber generally dispenses with separately specifying dynamics (for instance, bb. 10, 14, 138, 196). To be pointed out is Weber's, in part, odd slur placement in the overture, such as in the strings in bb. 9ff.: Such often contiguous and seemingly arbitrarily long slurs suggest playing only a consistent *sempre legato*. Weber's slurs sometimes placed only above the upper part (as in the place mentioned in the horns) mostly refer to instruments scored as pairs, sometimes also to parts notated beneath them, and are frequently to be understood as phrasing rather than articulation slurs. At the same time, such indications notated in the upper part of a group are applicable to all of its grouped parts (cf. bb. 209f. Vl. 1), without applying concurrently to other groups. It is the aim of this edition that very closely follows the source to make clear the effects to which Weber attaches great importance. This text corresponds to the text presented in the complete edition, together with a few careful performance-practice

IV

additions. The work's sources are freely acces-
sible on the website www.freischuetz-digital.de

Tim Hüttemeister
Joachim Veit
Translation: Margit L. McCorkle

VORWORT

Die Ouvertüre zu seiner dreiaktigen Oper *Der Freischütz* entstand – wie bei Weber üblich – als letzter Teil der Kompositionsarbeit (sieht man von der später eingelegten Romanze des Ännchen ab) im Mai 1820, also mehr als ein Jahr vor der Berliner Uraufführung des Werkes am 18. Juni 1821. Webers Geduld wurde durch die lange Wartezeit bis zur Berliner Premiere auf eine harte Probe gestellt, so dass er zwischenzeitlich in privaten Zirkeln bereits einzelne Nummern des Werks zur Aufführung brachte. Die Ouvertüre wurde dagegen sogar öffentlich aufgeführt: Im Sommer und Herbst 1820 nahm Weber die ausgeschriebenen Stimmen mit auf seine Reise, die ihn nach Norddeutschland und bis Kopenhagen führte. Nachweislich erklang sie bereits vor der Uraufführung der Oper in Halle, Kopenhagen, Hamburg, Braunschweig und Dresden.

Sieht man von dem (auch in Einzelnummern) vertriebenen Klavierauszug ab, ist die Ouvertüre der einzige Teil des Werks, der schon zu Webers Lebzeiten in gedrucktem Stimmenmaterial erhältlich war. Nach erfolglosen Verhandlungen mit Nikolaus Simrock schloss Weber im Oktober 1822 (zu diesem Zeitpunkt war die Oper schon an mehr als 40 Bühnen gegeben worden!) einen Verlagsvertrag mit Adolph Martin Schlesinger in Berlin und lieferte ihm noch im gleichen Monat die Stichvorlage ab. Die Stimmen erschienen Ende 1822.

Diese Stimmen sind neben dem Partiturautograph und acht erhaltenen, von Weber autorisierten Kopien des Werkes die relevanten Quellen der Ouvertüre. Da bei dem Stimmendruck nicht eindeutig festgestellt werden kann, welche Änderungen (vornehmlich im Bereich der Artikulation und Bogensetzung) auf den Komponisten zurückgehen, stellt das in der Staatsbibliothek zu Berlin erhaltene Autograph (Signatur: Mus. ms. autogr. C. M. v. Weber 7) die Hauptquelle für die Edition dar, die dieser Vorlage so getreu wie möglich folgt.

Die vorliegende Partitur versteht sich nicht als für die Praxis eingerichtete Ausgabe, sondern dokumentiert gemäß den Richtlinien der Weber-Gesamtausgabe neben den Notationsgepflogenheiten des Komponisten speziell bei der Bezeichnung der sekundären Schicht seine in vielen Fällen lückenhaften (etwa T. 61ff., 171ff. 202ff. oder 279ff.), stellvertretend nur in der Oberstimme notierten (z. B. T. 59ff., 209ff.) nicht eindeutigen (T. 243ff.) und gelegentlich auch widersprüchlichen Angaben (T.181ff., T. 209ff. Fl. u. Vl., T. 243ff. Bläser). Hier haben die Herausgeber nur sehr zurückhaltend eingegriffen, um die originale Notierung, die Weber als mit sehr feinen klanglichen Nuancen kalkulierenden Komponisten zeigt, weitgehend zu erhalten.

Ergänzungen, die die Herausgeber nach den übrigen Quellen vorgenommen haben, stehen in ( ), eigene Vorschläge in [ ]. Lediglich durch *colla parte*-Anweisung vermerkte Stimmen sind in den Zeichen ⌈ und ⌉ eingeschlossen. Die über dem Notentext gesetzten Markierungen bezeichnen einen Wechsel von linker zur rechten Seite ⊤ bzw. ein Umblättern im Autograph ⊤⌠ – in vielen Fällen wird dadurch deutlich, warum an solchen Stellen Einträge etwa zur Dynamik oder Artikulation unerwartet abbrechen. Im Falle von *Solo*-Bezeichnungen verzichtet Weber in der Regel auf eine separate Angabe der Dynamik (etwa T. 10, 14, 138, 196). Hinzuweisen ist auch auf Webers teils eigenartige Bogensetzung wie etwa in den Streichern in T. 9ff. der Ouvertüre: Solche, oft aneinander anschließenden und scheinbar willkürlich langen Bögen deuten lediglich ein dichtes *sempre-legato*-Spiel an. Webers manchmal nur über der oberen Stimme gesetzten Bögen (wie an der genannten Stelle in den Hörnern) beziehen sich meist auf beide, paarig besetzte Instrumente, teils auch auf in der Partitur darunter notierte Stimmen und sind häufig eher als Phrasierungs-, denn als Artikulationsbögen zu verstehen. Gleichzeitig können solche in der oberen Stimme einer Gruppe notierten Bezeichnungen für alle Stimmen einer Gruppe gültig sein (vgl. etwa T. 209f. Vl. 1), ohne zugleich zwingend für andere Gruppen mit zu gelten. Es ist Ziel der sehr eng der Quelle folgenden Edition, deutlich zu machen, auf welche Effekte Weber besonderen Wert legte. Der vorliegende Notentext entspricht dem in der Gesamtausgabe vorgelegten Text mit einigen wenigen behutsamen Ergänzungen für die Praxis. Die Quellen des Werkes stehen auf der Website www.freischuetz-digital.de zur freien Einsicht zur Verfügung.

Tim Hüttemeister
Joachim Veit

PRÉFACE

Weber composa l'ouverture de son opéra en trois actes *Der Freischütz* en mai 1820. Conformément à ses habitudes d'écriture, (hormis la romance d'Ännchen qui fut ajoutée par la suite), il s'agissait-là de la dernière étape de la composition de l'œuvre qui fut ainsi achevée plus d'un an avant sa création le 18 juin 1821 à Berlin. Sa patience mise à rude épreuve pendant cette longue attente, Weber finit par faire jouer entre temps certains numéros de son opéra en cercle privé. L'ouverture quant à elle, fut même donnée en public. En effet, au cours de l'été et de l'automne 1820, Weber en emporta le matériel au cours d'un voyage qui le mena de l'Allemagne du nord à Copenhague. Ainsi est-il attesté que l'ouverture fut donnée en public dès avant sa création, notamment dans les cités de Halle, Copenhague, Hambourg, Brunswick et Dresde.

Exceptée la réduction pour piano également mise en circulation (y compris en numéros séparés), l'ouverture est la seule partie de l'œuvre dont le matériel était disponible en version imprimée du vivant de Weber. En octobre 1822 (date à laquelle son opéra avait déjà été donné sur plus de 40 scènes !), après des tractations infructueuses avec Nikolaus Simrock, Weber conclut un accord avec l'éditeur Adolph Martin Schlesinger à Berlin et lui livra aussitôt la copie à graver. Le matériel d'orchestre parut à la fin de l'année 1822.

Ce matériel, ainsi que le manuscrit autographe de la partition et huit copies autorisées par Weber parvenues à la postérité, constituent les sources pertinentes relative à l'ouverture. Comme il n'est pas possible de déterminer précisément quelles modifications (en particulier dans le domaine de l'articulation et des liaisons) apportées lors de la publication du matériel sont attribuables au compositeur, le manuscrit conservé à la Staatsbibliothek zu Berlin (cote Mus. ms. autogr. C. M. v. Weber 7) constitue la source principale sur laquelle repose la présente édition qui s'y conforme aussi fidèlement que possible.

La présente partition n'est pas conçue comme une édition pratique. Conformément aux règles ayant présidé à l'édition complète des œuvres de Weber, elle documente non seulement les habitudes d'écriture du compositeur, mais aussi en particulier lors de la description de la couche secondaire, ses indications souvent lacunaires (par ex. M 61ss., 171ss. 202ss. ou 279ss.), présentes parfois uniquement dans la partie supérieure (par ex. M 59ss., 209ss.), ou confuses (M 243ss.), voire dans certains cas contradictoires (M 181ss., M 209ss. Fl. et Vl., M. 243ss. vents). Les éditeurs ne sont intervenus ici qu'avec beaucoup de retenue afin de rester au plus près de la notation originale qui révèle un Weber jouant avec des nuances sonores très subtiles.

Les ajouts apportés par les éditeurs d'après les autres sources figurent entre ( ), leurs suggestions personnelles entre [ ]. Seules les parties signalées par *colla parte* sont encadrées des signes ⌈ et ⌉. Les indications placées au-dessus de la partition signalent le passage de la page de gauche à la page de droite ⊤, voire une tourne dans le manuscrit autographe ⊤⌈ – dans de nombreux cas, cela permet de comprendre pourquoi les signes de dynamique ou d'articulation s'interrompent brutalement. Pour les parties marquées *Solo*, Weber renonce généralement à indiquer la dynamique séparément (notamment M 10, 14, 138, 196). Soulignons également le placement des liaisons parfois singulier de Weber, par ex. M 9ss. sur les cordes. Ce genre de liaisons souvent accolées bout à bout et de longueur apparemment arbitraire, indique uniquement un jeu dense, *sempre legato*. Parfois uniquement apposées au-dessus de la voix supérieure (comme à l'endroit indiqué pour les cors), les liaisons de Weber se rapportent généralement aux deux instruments notés par paires, voire également aux parties notées en dessous dans certains cas. Elles seront souvent considérées davantage comme des liaisons de phrasé plutôt que comme des liaisons d'articulation. De telles indications notées sur la partie supérieure d'un groupe peuvent aussi s'appliquer à toutes les

VIII

parties de ce groupe (cf. par ex. M 209s. Vl. 1), sans pour autant concerner les autres groupes. L'objectif de cette édition très fidèle à la source est de faire ressortir les effets les plus importants aux yeux de Weber. La partition présentée ici correspond à celle de l'édition complète des œuvres de Weber et comprend quelques rares ajouts effectués avec la plus grande prudence destinés à l'exécution. Les sources sont consultables librement sur le site www.freischuetz-digital.de.

Tim Hüttemeister
Joachim Veit
Traduction : Michaëla Rubi

DER FREISCHÜTZ

Overture

Carl Maria von Weber
(1786–1826)
WeV C.7

        EE 3702

2

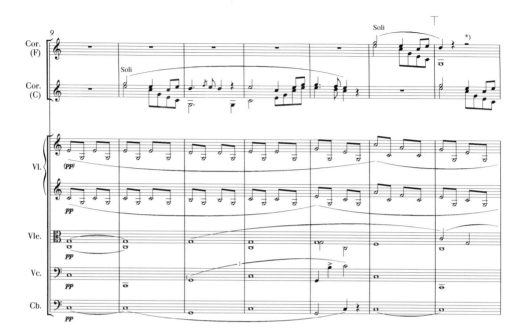

*) Nach Seitenwechsel im Autograph sind die Cor. nur lückenhaft bezeichnet, ohne dass ein *non-legato* intendiert ist.

4

8

11

*) Die Punkte deuten kein *Staccato*, sondern lediglich die Auflösung der Kürzelschreibweise in Achtelwerte an.

*) Streicher und Ob. (vermutlich auch Fg.) sollen offensichtlich *ff* beibehalten.
**) Die Haltebögen bezeichnen ein akzentfreies Tremolo und sind von Weber in der Regel (wie hier) nicht konsequent notiert.

14

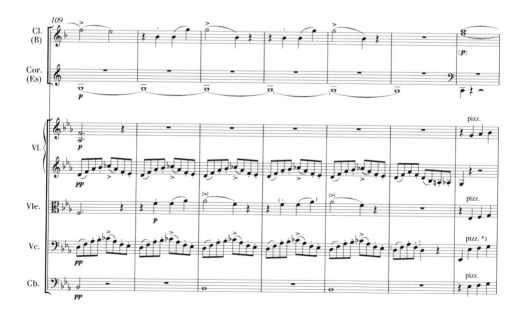

*) Im Autograph alle pizz.-Anweisungen am Taktstrich notiert, in den autorisierten Kopien ab 2. Note.

16

*) Die widersprüchliche Notierung der Dynamik (die nur teilweise eine Rücknahme nahelegt) findet sich so im Autograph.

*) Die im Autograph unklare Besetzung *a due* ist hier nach dem Stimmen-Erstdruck ergänzt.

20

21

*) Die widersprüchliche und uneinheitliche Artikulationsbezeichnung entspricht dem Autograph.

*) In Streichern und Bläsern ist eigenartigerweise in T. 181–190 keine generelle Rücknahme der Dynamik notiert.

24

30

*) Im Autograph ist die separate *Stringendo*-Anweisung in den Bässen schon mit Beginn von T. 228 notiert.

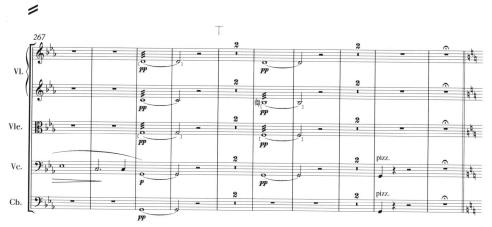

36

38

*) In T. 298 zweite Viertel in Vc. und Cb. in den autorisierten Quellen eindeutig *e*.